French Cuisine Cookbook

50 Easy and Delicious French Recipes

By

Patrick Smith

ISBN-10: 1500387924
ISBN-13: 978-1500387921

Contents

Section 1: Breakfast

1. French Breakfast Cinnamon Puffs

These muffins are easy and fast to make. They only require 5 minutes of preparation time and are ready in 30 minutes.

1 ½ cups **all-purpose flour**
1 ½ tsp **baking powder**
1/3 cup shortening
1 whole **egg**
¼ tsp **nutmeg**
½ tsp **salt**
½ cup **milk**
1 tsp ground **cinnamon**
½ cup **white sugar** (evenly divided)
6 tbs **margarine** (melted)

Makes 1 dozen puffs
Calories: 225 per serving

Preheat oven to 350°F (175°C). Line cups with paper muffin liners or grease muffin cups.

Combine flour, baking powder, nutmeg and salt in a bowl. In a separate bowl, whisk half of the sugar and shortening until smooth. Beat in the egg until blended.

Add flour mixture and milk to the sugar-shortening mixture. Stir until blended. Fill prepared cups or muffin cups with the batter.

Bake for about 23 minutes, or until golden brown. Meanwhile, mix remaining sugar and cinnamon in a bowl.

While still hot, dip the tops of the muffins into the melted margarine, then into the sugar-cinnamon mixture. Serve warm.

2. Pan Fried French Toast with Berry

This healthy breakfast uses 100% whole grain bread which ensures high fiber and protein. It takes less than 10 minutes to prepare.

1 **egg**
1 dash of **spice** of your choice
¼ cup **milk**
2 slices **whole grain bread**
1/4 cup frozen **berries**
Low fat **cooking spray**

Makes 2 slices
Calories: 118 per slice

In a bowl, whisk the egg with spice and milk. Stir until smooth. Heat non-stick pan over medium heat and add cooking spray. Dip bread in egg mixture and place in the pan. Cook for about 3 minutes on one slide and 1 minute on the other side, or until egg is well cooked.

Meanwhile, thaw berries in microwave for 30 seconds on high. Cut open center of toast and stuff berries into it. Serve immediately.

Enjoy!

3. French Classic Crepes

A classic great breakfast on weekends. It is easily prepared within
5 minutes and needs 30 minutes of cooking time.

1 cup all-purpose **flour**
¼ tsp **salt**
1 tsp **white sugar**
3 **eggs**
2 cups **milk**
2 tbs **butter** (melted)

Makes 12 servings
Calories: 103 per serving

In a bowl mix flour, salt and sugar until combined.

In a separate bowl, whisk eggs and milk using hand mixer until
smooth. Mix in the flour mixture until well incorporated. Stir in
butter and mix until a batter is formed.

Heat a greased skillet over medium-high heat. Scoop about 2 tbs
of the batter onto the skillet, tilting and rotating it to spread batter
as thinly as possible and cook until brown on both sides. Repeat to
make more crepes.

Serve rolled up and filled with fruit jam and/or whipped cream.

Enjoy!

4. French Toast with Blueberries

This blueberry breakfast can be prepared the night before. It takes 40 minutes to cook.

1 cup fresh or frozen **blueberries** (thawed)
10 slices **French bread** (diced)
3 oz. (85 g) **cream cheese** (diced)
½ cup all-purpose **flour**
½ cup **nuts** (chopped)
1 ½ cups **milk**
6 whole **eggs**
1 tbs **sugar**
½ tsp **vanilla**
Maple syrup (optional)
¼ tsp **salt**

Makes 8 servings
Calories: 220 per serving

Preheat oven to 400°F (200°C) and grease a baking dish.

Combine flour, salt, eggs, vanilla, and sugar in a bowl. Mix until smooth, then add bread cubes and toss to coat.

In a casserole, top bread mixture evenly with cream cheese, nuts and blueberries. Cover and chill for at least 1 hour, but less than a day.

Remove cover and bake for about 25 minutes, or until golden brown. Serve with maple syrup.

Enjoy!

5. Whole Wheat French Toast

Another way to enjoy a traditional French toast. It is ready to be enjoyed in less than 25 minutes.

8 slices **whole wheat bread**
¼ tsp **vanilla extract**
¾ cup low-fat **milk**
2 tsp **butter** (melted)
Maple syrup (optional)
2 large **egg whites**
1 large **egg**
Cinnamon to taste (optional)
Blue-, black-, and **raspberries** (optional)
Salt to taste

Serves: 4
Calories: 255 per serving

Preheat oven to 200°F (100°C).

In a bowl, beat milk, vanilla extract, egg whites, egg, and ½ tsp salt until smooth. Set aside.

In a nonstick pan, melt 1 tsp butter over medium heat. Coat bread slices on both sides with egg mixture, place a few slices in the pan and cook for about 7 minutes, or until lightly browned on both sides.

Transfer to the oven to keep toast warm. Add maple syrup and, optionally, berries and cinnamon.

Enjoy!

6. French Toast Stick with Cinnamon

2 slices **French bread** (cut into strips)
1/3 cup of beaten **egg**
1 tsp **Vanilla syrup**
Cinnamon to taste
Sweetener
¼ tsp **vanilla** extract

Makes 1 serving
Calories: 110 per serving

In a bowl, whisk egg with vanilla syrup and a bit of cinnamon.
Coat bread strips with egg mixture and cook in a pan for about 5
minutes, or until golden brown.

Drizzle sweetener and some more cinnamon on top. Serve plain,
or top with maple syrup, berries of your choice, or powdered
sugar.

Enjoy!

7. Potato Pancake with Cantal Cheese

This recipe is enjoyed in the coldest parts of France. It is easy to make with simple ingredients and is ready within 40 minutes.

5 oz. (140 g) lean **bacon** (cubed)
2 lbs. (900 g) baking **potatoes** (thinly sliced)
8 oz. (225 g) **Cantal cheese** (diced or cut into thin, narrow strips)
2 tbs **coconut oil** or **vegetable oil**
Salt and **pepper** to taste

Serves 4
Calories 225 per serving

In a skillet, heat bacon cubes over medium heat for about 3 minutes, or until fat begins to run, but not yet browned. Remove meat, drain fat and set aside.

In the same skillet, heat the oil of your choice, add potatoes and season with salt and pepper. Lower heat, cover and cook for about 5 minutes. Mix in the bacon, uncover and continue cooking over low heat for about 23 minutes. Stir frequently until potatoes are fork tender and browned.

Mix in cheese and season to taste. Level the potatoes by pressing down in the pan. Set heat to high and cook further for 4-5 minutes without stirring, until edges turn brown.

Turn off the heat, loosen the edges of the cake and transfer to a warmed platter. Serve hot.

Enjoy!

8. French Omelet with Tarragon and Chives

A delicious and easy to make omelet. Apart from tarragon and chives, you can also try other herbs you have available.

A few sprigs of **tarragon** and **chives** (finely chopped)
1 ½ tsp unsalted **butter**
3 large **eggs**
2 tsp **water**
1 dash of **salt**

Makes 1 omelet
Calories: 65 per serving

In a bowl, beat eggs with salt and water. Heat a nonstick pan over high heat. Spread butter and cook eggs until the edges begin to turn opaque. Lower heat and continue cooking until the omelet's underside is well cooked and the top is still slightly undercooked.

Using a heatproof spatula, fold in one third of the omelet over. Loosen the bottom of the omelet and slide the unfolded edge first onto a plate, then use the edge of the pan to flip the folded portion over the unfolded portion.

Garnish with chopped fresh herbs and serve immediately.

Enjoy!

9. French Toast with Egg Substitute

This is one of the best tasting and healthiest toasts I know. It is prepared in 5 minutes and needs about 8 minutes of cooking time. Choose coconut ingredients over others for maximum health benefits.

1 ¼ cups fat free **egg substitute**
1 slice **bread** (in small pieces)
1 tbs **raisins**
1 tbs **cinnamon**
3 tsp **coconut butter** or **butter**
1 tbs **coconut sugar** (or other sugar substitute)
2 tbs **water**
1 tsp **ginger** (optional)

Makes 2 servings
Calorie 75 per serving

In a bowl, combine cinnamon, the butter and sugar substitute of your choice, water, and raisins. Mix well until blended.

Transfer to a lightly greased skillet and cook over medium heat until the edges start to crisp and bubbles begin to form on top. Mix in bread and cook until your desired level of doneness.

Enjoy!

10. Macaroni-Cheese with Yogurt

This recipe tastes great and healthy for it uses whole wheat and lactose-free dairy. Cooks within 20 minutes.

10 oz. (285 g) whole wheat **macaroni**
2 cups **mozzarella cheese** (grated, divided)
1 tsp **paprika**
3 **eggs**
2 cups **Bulgarian yogurt**
1 oz. (30 g) **French dressing**

Makes 5 servings
Calories: 255 per serving

Preheat oven to 350°F (180°C).

In a pot, boil salted water and cook pasta until al dente.

In a bowl, mix yogurt, dressing and eggs. Add 1 cup cheese and mix until well incorporated. Transfer to a lightly greased baking dish, top with remaining cheese and drizzle with paprika.

Bake for about 20 minutes, or until firm. Serve with some fresh tomatoes.

Enjoy!

Section 2: Lunch

1. French Poutine with Mushroom Gravy

Crispy oven-fried potatoes topped with just enough sharp cheese and grease-free mushroom-filled gravy. It is ready in half an hour.

1 ½ lbs. (680 g) **baby potatoes** (quartered)
¼ cup **onion** (finely chopped)
½ cup **Cheddar cheese** (shredded)
2 tbs **chives** (finely chopped)
5 tsp **extra virgin olive oil** (divided)
3 tbs **all-purpose flour**
1 ½ cups **beef broth** or **mushroom broth** (divided)
1 cup **white mushrooms** (coarsely chopped)
¼ + 1/8 tsp **salt** (divided)
½ tsp **ground pepper** (equally divided)

Makes 4 servings
Calories: 235 per serving

Preheat oven to 450°F (230°C). Position the rack in lower third level.

In a large bowl, combine potatoes, ¼ teaspoon each salt and pepper, and 2 tsp olive oil, then toss to coat. Spread evenly on a baking dish, then bake for about 23 minutes, stirring once, until fork tender and lightly browned.

In a separate bowl, mix flour with ½ cup of your chosen broth. Set aside.

In a skillet, heat the remaining oil over medium heat. Add mushrooms and onion, then cook for about 6 minutes, stirring frequently, until it starts to brown. Add the remaining broth, lower heat and bring to a simmer. Cook for about 10 minutes, or until reduced by half its volume.

Add the reserved flour and broth mixture. Cook for 2 minutes, stirring continuously, until smooth and thickened. Stir in chives and the remaining salt and pepper.

When the potatoes are done, push them together in the center of the dish. Drizzle cheese, transfer to the oven and bake for 5 more minutes, or until the cheese is melted. Serve the potatoes with the gravy on top.

Enjoy!

2. Chicken Cordon Bleu I

Cordon Bleu is a delicious traditional French meal that has become very popular everywhere in the world. Preparation and cooking times are within 30 minutes each.

4 **chicken breast fillets** (skinned)
4 slices of **ham**
1 cup **bread crumbs**
4 slices of **cheese**
4 tbs **butter** (softened)
1 **egg** (beaten)
Salt and **pepper**

Makes 4 servings
Calories: 235 per serving

Preheat oven to 350°F (180°C)

On a flat surface, lay out the chicken breasts and drizzle some salt and pepper. Top each fillet with a slice each of cheese and ham. Roll up the fillets tightly. Secure edges with a toothpick.

Coat the rolls evenly with egg then with the bread crumbs. Place the rolls in a greased baking dish, seam side down, place 1 tbs of butter on top of each roll and bake for about 35 minutes.

Enjoy!

3. Poulet à la Kiev with Herbs

This is a delicious recipe for a poultry stuffed with herb butter. It is ready in less than an hour.

For the herb butter:
8 tbs **butter** (softened)
2 cloves **garlic** (finely minced)
2 tbs fresh **tarragon** (finely chopped)
2 tbs fresh **chives** (finely chopped)
2 tbs fresh **parsley** (finely chopped)
Juice of ½ **lemon**
¼ tsp **pepper**

For the Chicken:
4 **chicken breasts** (boneless, skinless)
1 cup fine **breadcrumbs**
1/3 cup all-purpose **flour**
1 **egg** (beaten)
Coconut oil for frying

Makes 4 servings
Calories: 215 per serving

In a bowl, combine all the ingredients for the herb butter and mix until well blended. Wrap the mixture with plastic, bring into a cylinder shape and chill until hardened.

Cut hardened herb butter into 8 equal portions, each piece as long as the breasts' width. Place a piece of herb butter at one end of each breast and roll the meat up tightly round it, tucking in the edges.

Prepare 3 shallow bowls for dipping: one with flour, one with the beaten egg, and one with the breadcrumbs.

Completely coat each roll in flour, then egg, and finally in breadcrumbs. Place the rolls on a plate and chill for about 1/2 hour before frying.

Fill a sturdy deep pan with oil and heat over high heat to about 375°F (190°C). Add rolls one at a time and fry for about 15 minutes, turning as needed with cooking tongs, until completely browned and well cooked through.

Place rolls on paper towel and serve immediately.

Enjoy

4. French Stew with Pork and Prunes

A delicious recipe for a perfect lunch, ready within 1 ½ hours. It is best served with rice and roasted carrots.

4 lbs. (1.8 kg) boneless **pork shoulder** (trimmed, cut)
1 cup tawny **port** (sweet fortified wine)
¼ cup **sherry vinegar** or **red-wine vinegar**
2 cups large **prunes** (pitted)
1 cup **shallots** (minced)
1 tsp dry **thyme** (minced)
1 ½ cups **beef broth**
2 tbs **coconut oil**
1 tbs **butter**
2 tbs **water**
2 tsp **arrowroot flour**
2 tsp fresh **ginger** (grated)
1 tsp **salt** (divided)
Ground **pepper** to taste

Makes 10 servings
Calories: 255 per serving

Preheat oven to 350°F (180°C).

Season the pork with salt and pepper.

In a large, oven-proof pot or slow cooker, heat 1 tbs oil and butter over medium heat. Add pork and cook in batches for about 5 minutes, or until browned on all sides. Transfer to a plate.

Place the remaining oil, shallots and ginger in the same pot and cook for about 4 minutes while stirring, until lightly browned. Bring to a simmer, then add thyme and vinegar. Return pork to the pot and cover.

Transfer the pot to the oven and bake for 1 ½ hours, or until the pork is tender. Remove from the oven, uncover and allow to cool for 15 minutes.

Combine port and prunes in a saucepan, then bring to a simmer and cook for 10 minutes. Skim visible fat from the stew, then add to port and prunes. Continue to cook for 10 more minutes over low heat.

In a small bowl, mix arrowroot flour with water. Set aside.

Transfer the pork and prunes to a bowl, leaving the sauce behind. Bring the sauce to a simmer. Add the arrowroot mixture, stirring until the sauce just coats the spoon. Mix in the pork, prunes and the remaining ½ tsp salt into the sauce and heat further for about 1 minute.

Enjoy!

5. Chicken Cordon Bleu II

This delicious recipe adds paprika and a creamy white wine sauce to the already excellent cordon bleu. It is ready to be indulged in an hour.

6 halves **chicken breast** (skinless, boneless)
6 slices **ham**
6 slices Swiss **cheese**
1 tsp **chicken bouillon** granules
3 tbs all-purpose **flour**
½ cup dry **white wine**
1 tbs **arrowroot flour**
1 tsp **paprika**
6 tbs **butter**
1 cup heavy **whipping cream**

Makes 6 servings
Calories 225 per serving

Lay chicken on a flat surface. Place a cheese and ham slice on each breast. Fold the edges of the chicken up and roll over the filling, then secure edges with toothpicks.

In a small bowl, mix paprika and flour, then coat the chicken pieces. Set aside.

In a pan, heat butter over medium-high heat. Cook chicken until browned on all sides. Mix in wine and bouillon. Set heat to low, cover, bring to simmer and cook for about 30 minutes, or until chicken is cooked through.

Remove toothpicks and transfer the breasts to serving plates. Meanwhile, in a small bowl, blend arrowroot flour with cream, then add the mix to the pan. Cook while stirring until thickened. Pour sauce over the chicken.

6. Roasted Vegetables in Balsamic Vinegar

The intense flavor of aged vinegar is a great way to enhance this dish. Serve with roasted chicken or beef for a delicious meal.

4 cups red **potatoes** (diced, unpeeled)
1 large red **onion** (sliced)
2 cups baby **carrots**
1 cup green **beans** (cut)
1 clove **garlic** (crushed, finely chopped)
2 tbs balsamic **vinegar**
1 tsp dried **thyme**
1 tsp dried **rosemary** (crushed)
1 tsp rubbed **sage**
4 tsp **olive oil**
¾ tsp **salt**
½ tsp ground **black pepper**

Makes 6 servings
Calories 205 per serving

Heat the oven to 400°F (200°C). Lightly oil a large roasting pan.

In a bowl, combine the vinegar, olive oil, herbs, onion, garlic, potatoes and carrots. Toss to coat.

Transfer to the roasting pan and roast for about 35 minutes, stirring every 10 minutes.

Add the green beans to the pan and roast for 10 more minutes. Transfer to a serving plate and season with salt and pepper.

Enjoy!

7. Lettuce and Green Pea Soup

A delicious French classic with additional ham and cheese pitas. It is prepared and cooked within 20 minutes.

10 oz. (280 g) **lettuce** (coarsely chopped)
10 oz. (280 g) frozen **peas**
1 medium **onion** (finely chopped)
14 oz. (400 g) **chicken broth**
2 tsp **butter**
1/8 tsp dried **thyme** leaves
1 cup **water**
½ cup fat-free skim **milk**
1 tbs fresh **lemon juice**
Chives (for garnish)
¾ tsp **salt**
1/8 tsp ground **black pepper**

Makes 4 servings
Calories: 115 per serving

In a saucepan, melt butter over medium heat. Add onion and cook for about 5 minutes, or until tender, stirring occasionally. Mix in chicken broth, peas, thyme, lettuce, salt, pepper, and 1 cup water. Bring to a boil over high heat. Set heat to low and simmer for about 5 minutes. Mix in milk.

In a blender, blend pea mixture in batches at low speed until smooth. Make sure steam can escape as you do so. Transfer each batch to a large bowl after blending.

Return soup to saucepan. Bring to a boil again, then mix in lemon juice and remove from heat. Transfer soup to serving bowl. Garnish with chives.

Enjoy!

8. Classic Cassoulet

A classic French country meal with beans and chicken. It takes 2 hours to prepare but is well worth the wait.

Ingredients for the stew:
4 slices thick-cut **bacon** (cut into strips)
15 oz. (425 g) small white **beans** (rinsed, drained)
3 lbs. (1.3 kg) **chicken** thighs (skin and excess fat removed)
1 ¼ lbs. (560 g) sweet Italian **sausage**
1 large **onion** (coarsely chopped)
1 tbs **garlic** (chopped)
1 ½ cup dry **white wine**
1 ¾ lbs. (800 g) **tomatoes** (diced)
1 tbs **rosemary** (chopped)
1 tbs **thyme** leaves (chopped)
½ tsp hot **red-pepper** flakes
2 large **yellow bell peppers** (cut into chunks)
½ cup **parsley** (chopped)
½ tsp **salt**

Ingredients for the topping:
2 tbs **olive oil**
2 cups coarse fresh **breadcrumbs**
½ cup **Parmesan cheese** (grated)
2 tsp fresh **thyme** (chopped)

Serves 8
Calories: 365 per serving

Preheat oven to 375°F (190°C).

In a slow cooker, cook bacon over medium heat until crisp.

Using the fat drippings, brown chicken and sausages in batches for 8 minutes per batch. Transfer to a roasting pan and bake in the oven for about 15 minutes.

While the meat is in the oven, sauté onion and garlic in the slow cooker, using the same fat drippings. Cook for 5-7 minutes, stirring frequently. Add wine and cook for 2 more minutes. Mix in beans, tomatoes, and remaining stew ingredients, then bring to a simmer.

Remove chicken and sausages from oven. Stir into bean mixture with any accumulated juices from the roasting pan. Sprinkle bacon bits on top. Cover and bake for another 45 minutes, until chicken is tender and well cooked.

Meanwhile, heat oil in a pan over medium heat, then add breadcrumbs. Cook for about 7 minutes, stirring until toasted. Allow to cool, then mix in cheese and thyme.

Spoon the stew onto plates. Sprinkle each serving with toasted-breadcrumb mixture.

Enjoy!

9. French Onion Soup with Brandy

This French classic soup is easy to make and very tasteful. The 40 minute cooking time is well worth the wait.

4 cups low-salt **beef stock**
4 **baguettes** (cut to fit ramekins)
1 cup **raclette cheese** (grated)
2 medium **onions** (finely chopped)
1 tbs unsalted **butter**
1 tbs **brandy**
Salt and ground **black pepper** to taste

Makes 4 servings
Per serving: 370 calories

Preheat oven to 450°F (230°C).

In a nonstick pan, cook onions for about 15 minutes over high heat, stirring continuously, or until soft and caramelized. Mix in butter and toss onions to coat. Remove from heat and stir in brandy.

Return to heat and continue cooking for about 30 seconds, until brandy is absorbed. Add beef stock, bring to a simmer and cook for about 5 minutes. Season with salt and pepper.

Divide soup among ramekins placed on a baking sheet. Top each with 1 or 2 slices of bread and ¼ cup cheese, then bake for 4-5 minutes, or until cheese is bubbly and browned in spots.

Enjoy!

10. Chicken Raclette Dish

These baked chicken breasts are made with a toasted coating of Dijon mustard, pine nuts and grated Parmigiano-Reggiano cheese. It only takes 15 minutes to prepare and is ready to be served after 1 hour.

4 half **chicken breasts** (trimmed, boneless, skinless)
1/3 cup of **pine nuts** (toasted, chopped)
1/3 cup **Parmigiano-Reggiano cheese** (grated)
Olive oil (for the baking dish)
4 tsp **Dijon mustard**
1 **garlic** clove (peeled)
1/8 cup **parsley leaves**
1 tsp **rosemary**

Makes 4 servings
Calories: 215 per serving

Preheat oven to 325°F (160°C).

In a bowl, combine nuts with cheese, garlic and herbs. Mix to blend.

Season top sides of each chicken breast with 1 tsp of the mustard, then sprinkle nut mixture over the tops.

Lightly grease a baking dish with olive oil. Arrange the breasts, coated side up, on the dish and top with the remaining nut mixture.

Bake for about 30 minutes, or until golden brown.

Enjoy!

Section 3: Dinner

1. Beaufort Cheese Cake

A heavenly light cheese soufflé made with Beaufort cheese. It is prepared in 15 minutes and ready to be served after 45 minutes.

2 oz. (60 g) **Beaufort cheese** (grated)
5 ½ tbs extra sifted **flour**
4 cups (1 liter) **milk**
4 whole **eggs** (separated)
4 tbs **butter**
A pinch of grated **nutmeg**
Salt and ground **pepper** (to taste)

Makes 4 servings
Calories: 215 per serving

Preheat oven to 375 °F (190°C). Lightly grease an oven proof soufflé dish.

In a nonstick pan, melt butter over medium heat. Turn off heat and slowly stir in flour until well mixed. Add the cold milk, while stirring. Season with salt and pepper. Add a pinch of nutmeg and whisk for a few minutes until mixture is smooth and thick.

In a separate bowl, whip egg whites, until stiff cones form. Beat in egg yolks and 6 tbs of the grated cheese. Mix until blended.

Pour the flour mixture into the prepared soufflé dish and fold in whipped egg mixture. Sprinkle top with remaining grated cheese.

Bake for about 30 minutes and then serve at once.

Enjoy!

2. Coq au Vin in White Wine

This French classic recipe uses white wine to step up flavor and make a tenderizing marinade for the chicken.

Marinade:
6 lbs. (2.7 kg) **chicken** pieces (drumsticks, thighs, breasts)
8 whole black **pepper corns**
1 cup **onion** (chopped)
½ cup **carrot** (sliced)
2 tbs **olive oil**
3 cups dry **white wine**
½ cup **celery** (sliced)
3 cloves **garlic** (chopped)
2 tbs fresh whole **parsley** leaves
½ tsp **salt**

Coq au Vin:
1 lbs. (450g) small **red potatoes**
4 slices **bacon** (chopped)
1 tbs **olive oil**
12 small **white onions** (peeled)
3 cloves **garlic** (chopped)
1 **shallot** (chopped)
5 medium **carrots** (peeled, cut)
2 stalks **celery** (sliced)
3 cups **chicken broth**
1 tbs balsamic **vinegar**
¼ cup **all-purpose flour**
1 tsp **thyme** leaves (chopped)
1 **bay leaf**
½ tsp **salt**
¼ tsp ground **black pepper**

Serves: 6
Calories: 455 per serving

In a large sauce pan, combine all ingredients for marinade, except chicken. Bring to a boil and simmer over a lower heat for about 5 minutes. Turn off heat and set aside to cool.

Place chicken parts in a glass container with lid. Mix in marinade and toss to coat. Cover and chill for at least 3 ½ hours or overnight.

Remove chicken parts from marinade and pat off excess sauce. Strain marinade, discard solids and reserve the liquid.

In a large slow cooker, cook bacon over medium heat until crisp. Transfer to paper towels, leaving the fat drippings in the cooker. Place chicken parts in the cooker and cook until brown. Transfer to a platter.

Discard all but 1 tbs fat. Stir in olive oil and sauté onions for about 10 minutes until lightly browned. Add garlic, shallot, carrots, and celery. Sauté for another 5 minutes.

Meanwhile, in a mixing bowl, combine the reserved marinade liquid and flour. Mix well to blend. Add mixture to the slow cooker with the bay leaf, chicken broth, vinegar, thyme, salt, and pepper.

Return chicken to slow cooker, cover and cook for about 45 minutes. Mix in potatoes and cook for another 20 minutes, or until potatoes are fork-tender. Transfer to serving bowls, garnish each with reserved bacon bits and serve.

Enjoy!

3. Lemony Chicken

This chicken recipe is a delicious and easy to prepare dish. It is ready in 20 minutes.

4 chicken **breast** halves (boneless, skinless)
1 whole **egg** (beaten)
1 ½ cups **chicken broth**
Juice of 1 medium **lemon**
1 tbs **parsley** (chopped)
1 cup **flour**
1 tbs **butter**
1 tsp **paprika**
1 tbs **olive oil**
Salt (optional)

Makes 4 servings
Calories: 125 per serving

In a bowl, combine flour and paprika.

In another bowl, combine half of the lemon juice and the beaten egg. Whisk to blend.

Coat chicken breasts with flour mixture, dip into the egg mixture and coat again with the flour mixture.

In a non-stick pan, heat butter and oil over medium heat. Fry chicken breasts for about 4 minutes, or until golden brown on all sides.

Add chicken broth and the remaining lemon juice to the pan. Cover and simmer for about 7 minutes. Add parsley, turn off heat and season with salt, if desired.

Enjoy!

4. Triple Cheese Spinach Quiche

This is a crust-less quiche recipe with spinach and cheeses. The preparation time is 15 minutes; the cooking time is 40 minutes.

10 ½ oz. (300g) **spinach** (chopped)
½ cup **milk**
½ cup **whipping cream**
1 medium **onion** (chopped)
1 cup **mozzarella cheese** (shredded)
¼ cup **parmesan cheese** (shredded)
¼ cup **cheddar cheese** (shredded)
1 tbs **sun flower seeds**
4 whole **eggs**
1 tbs **olive oil**
1 tbs **butter**
1 clove **garlic** (minced)
¼ tsp **nutmeg**
Salt and **pepper**

Makes 7 servings
Calories: 325 per serving

Preheat oven to 325°F (162°C). Lightly oil a 9 inch (23 cm) quiche pan or pie pan.
In a frying pan, heat olive oil and butter over medium heat. Sauté onion and garlic until soft and translucent. Stir in spinach and cook for another 10 minutes.

In a large bowl, whip eggs with milk and whipping cream. Season with salt, pepper, and nutmeg. Add sunflower seeds, parmesan, spinach, and mozzarella. Mix well to blend. Transfer to the quiche pan or pie pan.

Drizzle cheddar cheese on top and bake for 30 minutes, or until toothpick comes out clean when inserted. Cool for 10 minutes before slicing into preferred cuts.

5. Flounder with Paprika and Herbs

This flounder dish is perfect if time is short. It is done in as little as 12 minutes.

2 lbs. (900 g) **flounder fillets** (patted dry)
½ cup **milk**
½ tsp **Hungarian paprika**
2 tbs **thyme** leaves
3 tbs **chives** (chopped)
1 tbs **dill** weed
4 tbs **butter**
Sea salt and **black pepper** to taste

Makes 4 servings
Calories, 115 per serving

Preheat oven to 350°F (175°C).

Arrange fish in a single layer on a shallow baking dish. Drizzle fish with a little salt and paprika. Sprinkle herbs and scatter butter all over. Add milk, covering half of the fish.

Bake for about 11 minutes or until fish is flakey. Season with salt and black pepper, if desired.

Enjoy!

6. Leek and Gruyère Quiche

This quiche takes 40 minutes to make and is best served with green salad on the side.

2 large **leeks** (sliced)
1 **onion** (sliced finely)
4 **eggs**
1 cup light **Gruyère** (grated)
½ cup **coffee** cream
2 tbs **olive oil**
2 tbs **flour**
1/8 tsp **nutmeg** (ground)
1 pinch smoky **paprika**
1 tbs **Dijon mustard**
1 pinch dry **thyme**
Salt and **pepper** to taste

Makes 6 servings
Calories: 215 per serving

Preheat oven to 375°F (190°C). Oil a 9 inch (23 cm) pie pan or quiche pan.

In a non-stick skillet, heat oil over medium heat and sauté leeks and onion until tender. Season with salt and pepper.

In a bowl, whisk eggs, flour, coffee cream, Gruyère, herbs and seasonings until well blended. Transfer to prepared pie pan or quiche pan. Mix in sautéed vegetables. Drizzle some grated cheese on top.

Bring water to a boil in a large pan and add the Gruyère mix. Ensure the bottom half of the mix is covered by water. Bake for about 40 minutes, or until light brown. Remove from water and cool on a wire rack.

7. Coq Au Vin Chicken with Potatoes

This version of Coq Au Vin only has a fraction of the calories it normally contains.

2 lb. (900 g) **chicken** pieces (boneless, skinless)
4 cups **white mushrooms** (quartered)
2 cups **potatoes** (in bite size pieces)
2 cup dry **red wine**
¼ cup **whole wheat flour**
Olive oil cooking spray
1 yellow **onion** (chopped)
1 **carrot** (peeled, sliced)
1 ½ cups low sodium **chicken broth**
1 tsp **Herbes de Provence**
1/2 tbs low sodium **tomato paste**
2 tbs fresh **parsley** (chopped)
¼ tsp each **sea salt** and ground **pepper**

Makes 6 servings
Calories: 257 per serving

In a large bowl, combine flour, with salt and pepper. Coat the chicken with the mixture. Heat a greased sauce pan over medium heat and fry chicken for about 5 minutes, turning once, until lightly browned. Transfer onto a platter.

On the same heated pan, stir fry mushrooms, carrot, and onion, then cook for about 4 minutes. Mix in wine, potatoes, tomato paste, broth, and Herbes de Provence. Return chicken and its juices to the pan, arrange in a single layer and bring to a boil. Lower heat, cover and simmer for about 20 minutes, or until the potatoes are fork tender and the chicken is well cooked through.

Transfer chicken and vegetables to shallow bowls. Boil sauce for about 4 minutes, or until it is reduced to about 1 ½ cups. Mix in parsley and pour sauce over chicken and vegetables.

8. Old-fashioned Ratatouille

Ratatouille is a well-known French stewed vegetable dish. It is done in less than an hour.

1 large **eggplant** (trimmed and diced)
2 medium **zucchini** (trimmed and diced)
1 medium **onion** (diced)
2 large fresh **tomatoes** (chopped)
2 cloves **garlic** (minced)
3 tbs **olive oil**
½ tsp dried **thyme**
¼ cup fresh **basil** (chopped)
¼ tsp dried **rosemary**
¼ tsp dried **marjoram**
¾ tsp **salt**
½ tsp ground **black pepper**

Makes 4 servings
Calories: 180 per serving

In a large nonstick sauce pan, heat 1 tbs olive oil over medium-high heat. Add the eggplant and stir cook for about 5 minutes, or until softened. Set aside.

Add the onion and another tbs of oil in the same heated pan. Sauté for about 5 minutes until softened and translucent. Stir in the zucchini and garlic and stir cook for 7 more minutes, or until softened.

Return the eggplant to the pan and stir in Herbes de Provence, tomatoes, salt and pepper to taste. Simmer for about 10 minutes. Mix in basil and the remaining tbs of oil.

Enjoy!

9. Beef and Mushroom Bourguignon

The classic French beef bourguignon gets a vegetarian twist. It cooks for about 2 hours.

1 ½ lbs. (680 g) top round **steak** (cubed)
2 cups   low-sodium **beef stock**
½ lb. (225 g) small button **mushrooms**
18 pearl **onions**
4 tsp **olive oil**
¼ cup + 2 tbs all-purpose **flour**
2 cups   + ½ cup **burgundy** or **pinot noir**
2 cups **water**
¼ tsp dried **orange peel**
1 **bay** leaf
1 tsp dried **thyme**
1 tsp **tomato paste**
1 large   **tomato**
2 cloves **garlic**
1 tsp **butter**
½ tsp **salt**
¼ tsp **black pepper** (ground)

Makes 6 servings
Calories: 315 per serving

Preheat oven to 350°F (175°C).

In a bowl, place flour and add beef cubes in batches. Toss to coat. Pat off any excess flour.

In a large non-stick pan, heat 1 tsp olive oil over medium heat. Fry the cubed stake in batches until browned. Transfer to an oven-proof pot. Add the wine, bay leaf, garlic cloves, beef stock, 1 cup water, orange peel, tomato, thyme, and tomato paste. Cover and simmer in the oven for about 90 minutes, stirring occasionally.

Meanwhile, combine 1 tsp olive oil, mushrooms, and pearl onions in the pan and sauté for about 5 minutes. Set aside.

Remove the beef stew from the oven and pour through a colander, capturing the liquid. Transfer the beef to a bowl and return the liquid to the pot. Add the remaining water and wine, then bring to a simmer.

Make beurre manié (kneaded butter) by blending softened butter and flour until smooth. Use to thicken the sauce to desired consistency. Season with salt and pepper.

Enjoy!

10. Scallops with Arugula à La Provençal

Scallops are not only tasty but healthy and economical. This recipe calls for herbs of your own choice, for which I suggest chives, parsley, basil, or a combination of them.

1 lb. (450 g) sea **scallops**
5 cups **cherry tomatoes**
3 + 2 tsp fresh **thyme** (chopped, divided)
2 + ½ tbs **garlic** (chopped, divided)
3 + 2 tsp **olive oil** (divided)
2 cups fresh **corn**
2 tsp **balsamic vinegar**
2 +1 tbs **herbs of your choice** (chopped, divided)
2 cups **arugula**
¼ + ¼ tsp **salt** (divided)
¼ + ¼ tsp ground **pepper** (divided)

Makes 4 servings
Calories: 222 per serving

Heat oven to 375°F (190°C). Coat a baking dish with cooking spray.

In a bowl, combine 3 tsp olive oil, 2 tbs garlic, 3 tsp thyme, ¼ tsp each of salt and pepper. Mix well, then transfer the mixture to the prepared dish.

Bake for about 23 minutes, stirring once, until tomatoes are tender. Stir corn into the tomato mixture.

In the same bowl as before, combine scallops with remaining oil, garlic, thyme, and salt and pepper. Add this mix on top of tomato mixture and continue baking for about 15 minutes, until scallops are cooked through.

Transfer only the scallops to a plate and cut them in halves.

Add vinegar and 2 tbs of your chosen herbs to the tomato mixture. Divide arugula, the tomato mixture and scallops among 4 serving bowls and top with remaining herbs.

Enjoy!

Section 4: Side Dishes

1. Classic French Fries

No French recipe archive would be complete without this all-time classic.

3 large baking **potatoes** (peeled)
1 tbs fresh **parsley** (chopped)
3 tbs **coconut oil**
Salt and ground **pepper**

Makes 6 servings
Calories: 105 per serving

Preheat oven to 425°F (220°C).

Peel slice the potatoes into the shape of fries. Combine the fries and coconut oil in a bowl until evenly coated.

Place the fries on one to two baking sheets and bake for about 30 minutes, turning sides after 15 minutes. At that point, they should be golden brown.

Drizzle with salt, pepper and parsley.

Enjoy!

2. Classic Galette

Galette is a classic country meal that goes very well with chicken and a small salad.

2 large russet **potatoes** (peeled, thinly sliced)
2 large sprigs **thyme**
2 tbs **butter**
Salt and ground **pepper**

Makes 4 servings
Calories: 135 per serving

Preheat oven to 400°F (200°C).

In a large oven-proof pan, heat butter over medium heat, then add 1 sprig of thyme at the center. Place potato slices to form an overlapping spiral in the pan. Season with salt and pepper. Cover and cook for about 8 minutes, or until golden brown.

Transfer the galette to a flat dish. Place another sprig of thyme at the center of the pan, carefully turn the galette around and transfer back to the pan. Season with salt and pepper.

Place pan in the oven and bake for 25 minutes, or until top side is browned. Gently transfer galette to the flat dish, cut into wedges, and serve immediately.

Enjoy!

3. Cheesy Aligot

A recipe for mashed potatoes with garlic, cream, and cheddar. It is ready in 45 minutes.

3 lb. (1.36 kg) **potatoes** (peeled, cubed)
3 cups **cheddar cheese** (grated)
1 clove **garlic** (crushed)
3 tbs **crème fraiche**
1/8 tsp **white pepper** (ground)
4 tbs **butter**
¾ tsp **salt**

Makes 10 servings
Calories: 215 per serving

In a pot of boiling water, cook potatoes for about 20 minutes, or until tender. Remove and mash potatoes in a mixer, adding butter, salt, and pepper, until the mixture is starts to become fluffy. Set aside.

In a skillet, heat crème fraiche and garlic over medium heat until it is about to steam. Transfer to a pot and add the potato mix. Set to low heat and whisk the mixture until blended.

Set heat to medium and gradually mix in the cheese. Continue whisking the mixture for about 10-12 minutes, until it gets a very smooth texture. Transfer to plates and serve immediately.

Enjoy!

4. Apple Cinnamon Carrots

This recipe features baby carrots coated in cinnamon and apple cider. It is ready in just about 30 minutes.

2 cups baking **apples** (chopped)
¾ lb. (340 g) **carrots** (sliced)
½ cup **apple cider**
2 tbs **butter**
1/3 cup **water**
¼ tsp **cinnamon**

Makes 6 servings.
Calories: 215 per serving

In a large pan, heat butter over low heat until it turns light brown. Remove from heat and allow to cool for 3 minutes.

Add water, apple cider, and cinnamon, then bring to boil over medium heat. Lower heat and simmer for 2 minutes.

Add carrots, cover and stir cook for another 10 minutes over medium heat. Add in apples and cook for another 5 minutes, until everything is tender.

Enjoy!

5. Green Beans with Garlic

This green bean side dish is a quick and very easy to make.

½ lb. (225 g) **green beans** (trimmed)
1 cup **parsley** leaves
1/3 cup **almonds** (toasted, chopped)
1 large clove **garlic**
1/3 cup extra-**virgin olive oil**
½ tsp **salt**

Makes 7 servings
Calories: 120 per serving

Fill a large saucepan with salted water. Bring to a boil over high heat, add the beans and cook for about 3-4 minutes. Drain and transfer beans to a bowl. Set aside and allow to cool.

In a blender, combine parsley, garlic, olive oil, and salt. Blend until the mix is smooth. Add almonds and continue blending until they are finely chopped and well incorporated.

Transfer the puree to the bowl with the beans, then toss to coat. Serve immediately.

Enjoy!

6. French Peas

This is an unforgettable pea dish with deli ham and a shallot. It is ready in 20 minutes.

1 lb. (450 g) frozen **peas** (thawed)
2 ½ oz. (70 g) **deli ham** (cubed)
1 tbs **chervil** (chopped)
1 **shallot** (finely diced)
½ tbs **butter** or **coconut butter**
¼ cup **water**
¼ cup **heavy cream**
Salt and **Pepper**

Makes 5 servings
Calories: 125 per serving

In a large pan, melt the butter over medium heat and sauté the shallot for about 2 minutes, or until tender. Stir in deli ham, add salt and pepper, and cook 1 additional minute. Add in peas and water, cover and set heat to low. Cook for 10 more minutes.

Uncover, add in cream, salt and pepper to taste and continue cooking for another 3 minutes, or until mixture thickens. Add chervil, some pepper, and serve at once.

Enjoy!

7. Sweet French Turnip

Turnips are fantastic vegetables and taste well no matter how you prepare them. This is a very simple but flavorful dish. It takes about 30 minutes to make.

8 fresh **turnips** (sliced)
2 tbs **butter** or **coconut butter**
1 tsp **basil** (optional)
2 tbs **sugar** (optional)

Makes 5 servings
Calories, 58 per serving

In a pot of boiling water, cook turnips for about 5 minutes, or until tender. Remove water.

In a skillet, heat the butter of your choice over medium heat, then add turnips. Sprinkle sugar if desired and cook for about 8 minutes, mixing intermittently until sugar caramelizes. Finally, add basil if desired.

Enjoy!

8. Ragoût with Potatoes and Carrots

This delicious ragoût is a bit more complex than other side dishes but well worth it.

1 ½ lbs. (680 g) **carrots** (cut into sticks)
12 oz. (340 g) **potatoes** (halved)
¾ cup fresh **peas**
1 tsp. **balsamic vinegar**
3 tbs **butter** or **coconut butter**
2 tbs **olive oil**
1 cup **brown chicken stock**
1 tsp. **garlic** (minced)
1 tsp each **lemon juice** and **zest** (finely grated)
2 oz. (60 g) **baby spinach** leaves
2 tsp. **tarragon** (chopped)
Salt

Makes 5 servings
Calories: 198 per serving

In a small bowl, whisk together vinegar, lemon juice, lemon zest, and 1 tbs water. Set aside.

In a large pan, heat 1 tbs each of the olive oil and your chosen butter over low heat.
Mix in carrots and ¾ tsp salt. Cover and stir cook for about 18-20 minutes, or until the carrots are just softened. Transfer carrots to a large plate. Set aside.

Add another 1 tbs of butter and olive oil to the fat in the pan. Place the halved potatoes in the pan, cut sides facing down.

Season with ¾ teaspoon of salt. Cover partially and cook for 5 minutes without stirring, or until the potatoes are browned.

Add the chicken stock and bring to a boil. Reduce heat, cover partially and simmer for about 5 minutes, or until the potatoes are tender. Add garlic to the potatoes and cook for about 1 minute, slowly stirring.

Add the lemon mixture, baby spinach, peas, and carrots. Stir cook for 1-2 more minutes. Remove from heat, then stir in the remaining butter and tarragon. Transfer to plates and serve immediately.

Enjoy!

9. Carrots with Tarragon

Tarragon deliciously offsets the sweetness of carrots in this classic French side dish. It is superb in combination with a large number of main dishes.

1 lb. (450 g) **carrots** (cut)
2 tbs **tarragon** (finely chopped)
3 tbs **butter** or **coconut butter**
2 cups **water**
½ tsp **sea salt** and to taste

Makes 4 servings
Calories: 122 per serving

Place carrot cuts in a large saucepan. Add your chosen butter, seal salt, and water. Make sure the water just covers carrots. Bring to a boil over high heat and cook for 10 minutes, shaking the pan intermittently, until the liquid begins to turn syrupy.

Turn off the heat, add the tarragon and stir until well combined. Season with salt to taste and serve immediately.

Enjoy!

10. Thyme Leeks and White Wine

2 lb. (900 g) **leeks** (halved lengthwise)
¼ cup **olive oil**
10 sprigs **thyme**
1 tbs dry **white wine**
½ tsp **sea salt**

Makes 4 servings
Calories: 165 per serving

Position rack in the center of the oven. Preheat to 350°F (180°C).

Place the leeks on a shallow baking dish, cut side down. Sprinkle thyme sprigs on top.

In a bowl, combine the olive oil, white wine of your choice, and 1 tbs water, then drizzle both the mix and salt over the leeks. Cover the baking dish tightly with tin foil and transfer to the rack.

Bake leeks for about 45 minutes, until fork tender. Remove cover and continue cooking for 15 more minutes. Remove thyme sprigs and serve warm.

Enjoy!

Section 5: Snacks and Treats

1. French Apple Yogurt

A delicious and nutritious snack that is ready within 25 minutes.

½ cup **apple juice**
3 large **apples** (diced)
2 cups plain **yogurt**
1 **cinnamon** stick
1 tbs **vanilla extract**

Makes 8 servings
Calories: 65 per serving

In a small pot, boil the apple juice and cinnamon stick over medium heat. Add the apple pieces and cook for about 10 more minutes. Remove the apple pieces and reserve 2 tbs of the liquid, then discard the cinnamon stick.

Save 1 cup of the cooked apples, then place the rest and the saved liquid into blender. Add 1 cup of yogurt and the vanilla extract. Mix until almost pureed. Transfer to a bowl and add the saved apple pieces and remaining yogurt.

Enjoy!

2. French Creamy Pancakes

These are a low-carb pancakes that are prepared and cooked in less than 10 minutes.

2 oz. (56 g) **cream cheese**
2 dashes of **cinnamon**
1 tsp **vanilla extract**
1 tbs **butter** or **coconut butter**
1 large **egg**
1 tsp **sweetener**

Makes 1 serving
Calories 127 per serving

In a bowl, whisk the egg with cream cheese, sweetener, 1 dash of cinnamon, and vanilla extract until well blended.

Heat a greased skillet over medium heat, add some of the batter and cook for about 4 minutes. Flip carefully with a spatula and cook for another 4 minutes. Transfer to a plate.

In a small microwavable bowl, melt 1 tbs of your chosen butter, add the remaining dash of cinnamon and pour over pancakes.

Enjoy!

3. Chocolaty Meringues

These meringues are perfect as treats or on top of cakes. They are ready in 90 minutes.

1 pinch **cream of tartar**
¼ cup **Nutella** or **Chocolate** (melted)
3 **egg** whites
1 pinch of **salt**
1/3 cup **sugar**

Number of Servings: 25
Calories: 20 per serving

Preheat the oven to 300°F (150°C). Position racks in the bottom third and one in the upper third of the oven. Line 2 baking sheets with parchment paper and set aside.

In a mixing bowl, whip egg whites, salt, and cream of tartar until soft peaks begin to form. Set mixer speed to high and gradually add sugar. Continue beating until stiff peaks begin to form.

Warm up the Nutella or chocolate in a pot until it becomes slightly liquid. Transfer the chocolate to the mixing bowl and use a spatula to gently fold it in. Do not mix it too much, or the mixture may not work as desired.

With a spoon, transfer 25 batches to the prepared oven racks and bake for 10 minutes, then lower heat to 200°F (90°C) and switch the position of the racks. Bake for 1 more hour, or until meringues are completely dried.

Enjoy!

4. Avocado Toasts with Tomatoes

Avocado and tomatoes are great combination for a healthy snack. This one takes about 20 minutes to make.

5 oz. (140 g) **baguette** (sliced into 15 slices)
2 cups **grape tomatoes** (quartered)
1 **avocado** (pitted, halved)
2 tbs **olive oil**
1 tsp **lemon juice**
Salt and ground **pepper** to taste

Makes 15 servings
Calories: 98 per serving

Preheat oven to 350 °F (180°C).

Brush bread slices on both sides with olive oil and bake for about 8 minutes on a baking sheet until golden.

Scoop the avocado flesh into a bowl, then add lemon juice and mash. Season with salt and pepper to taste. Spread on toasted bread. Serve topped with quartered grape tomatoes.

Enjoy!

5. Baked Baguette with Mushrooms

This is a quick and easy snack that can be enjoyed any time of the day. It also works well for breakfast.

1 **baguette** (sliced)
¼ lb. **Gruyère cheese** (shredded)
1 lb. **mushrooms** of your choice (sliced)
2 tbs **olive oil** or **coconut oil**
1 **yellow onion** (thinly sliced)
1 clove **garlic** (chopped)
1 tbs **thyme**
Salt and **pepper**

Makes 20 slices
Calories: 84 per slice

Preheat broiler to 400°F (200°C). Slice the baguette into 20 slices, place on a baking sheet and set aside.

Heat your chosen oil in a pan over medium heat. Add the yellow onion and garlic and cook for about 5 minutes. Add thyme and your chosen mushrooms and continue cooking for 10 minutes, or until softened. Season with salt and pepper to taste.

Before the mushrooms are done, place the baking sheet with baguette slices in the oven and broil for 2 minutes, or until browned.

Top baguette pieces with cooked mushroom mixture and Gruyère cheese, then broil for another 2 minutes.

Enjoy!

6. Tomato Bruschetta with Basil

A fresh and delicious French snack or appetizer.

1 **baguette** (cut into diagonal slices)
8 tbs **butter** or **coconut butter**
2 cups yellow grape **tomatoes** (halved)
2 cups red grape **tomatoes** (halved)
5 cloves **garlic** (finely minced)
15 **basil** leaves
1 tbs balsamic **vinegar**
2 tbs **olive oil**
Salt and **pepper** to taste

Makes 12 servings
Calories: 95 per serving

In a small pan, heat oil over medium-high heat. Fry garlic for about 1 minute, or until golden brown. Transfer to a mixing bowl and allow to cool slightly.

Add vinegar, basil, tomatoes, salt and pepper to the bowl. Toss to mix, then cover and chill for 1 hour.

In a large pan, melt half of your chosen butter and toast half of the baguette on both sides until golden brown. Repeat process with the other half of the butter and baguette.

Spoon tomatoes on the baguette slices and top with toasted garlic.

Enjoy!

7. French Mousse

A classic dessert that is ready in 30 minutes. You may need some practice to get it right, but once you do it is a star among party desserts.

6 oz. (170 g) **baking chocolate** (chopped)
3 **eggs** (separated)
¼ cup + 2 tbs **sugar** (divided)
3 tbs **butter** or **coconut butter**
½ tsp **cream of tartar**
½ cup **heavy cream** (cold)
½ tsp **vanilla extract**
Chocolate shavings (optional)
Whipped cream (optional)

Makes 4 servings
Calories: 135 per serving

Place a heatproof bowl over a saucepan containing hot water. Melt chocolate and your chosen butter in the bowl, then stir until smooth. Remove from heat and allow to cool slightly.

Add egg yolks to the chocolate, then whisk until smooth. Set aside.

In another bowl, whip egg whites until foamy. Add cream of tartar. Gradually whisk in ¼ cup sugar and beat until stiff peaks form.

Into a chilled bowl, whip heavy cream until thickened and foamy. Add the vanilla extract and remaining sugar. Continue whipping until soft peaks begin to form.

Slowly fold the egg whites into the chocolate mixture, then fold in the whipped cream. Ensure not to over mix the mousse or it may not work as desired. Divide mousse into 4 individual glasses, cover and refrigerate for several hours. Optionally, garnish with whipped cream and chocolate shavings before serving.

8. French Coconut Pie

A very easy but delicious pie overflowing with coconut flavor. The total baking time is 1 hour.

1 (10-inch / 25 cm) unbaked **pie shell**
13 ½ oz. (100 g) shredded **coconut**
2 **eggs** (beaten)
1 cup **milk**
4 tbs **butter** or **coconut butter** (melted)
1 tbs **all-purpose flour**
¾ cup **sugar**

Makes 7 servings
Calories: 140 per serving

Preheat oven to 350°F (175°C).

Melt the butter of your choice.

In a large bowl, beat eggs with melted butter until smooth. Add the flour, sugar, shredded coconut, and milk. Mix until well blended.

Evenly spread into the pie shell and bake for about 1 hour until firm.

Enjoy!

9. Grilled Gruyère and Ham Sandwich

This is a much loved French street sandwich that has a crispy exterior filled with ham and Gruyère cheese.

8 slices **white bread**
4 slices **Gruyère cheese**
4 slices of **ham**
2 **eggs**
4 tbs **heavy cream**
1 tbs **butter** or **coconut butter**
Salt, **pepper**, and **herbs de Provence**

Makes 4 servings
Calories: 145 per serving

In a bowl, beat eggs with heavy cream, then add salt, pepper and herbs de Provence. Coat the white bread with this mixture.

Sandwich 1 slice of cheese and ham between 2 slices of bread. Place each sandwich in a hot frying pan, cover and simmer both sides on low heat for about 10 minutes. Repeat cooking for remaining sandwiches.

Enjoy!

10. French Tapenade

Tapenade is a popular food in the south of France, where it is eaten on bread. It is effortless to make.

3 ½ oz. (100 g) **green olives** (stoned)
4 slices **bread**
2 tbs **capers**
1 clove **garlic**
6 tbs **olive oil**

Makes 4 serving
Calories: 185 per serving

Combine capers, garlic, can olives in a blender. While blending, slowly pour the olive oil into the mix. Transfer to a plate and spread on bread slices. Alternatively, transfer to a jar and top with oil film for preservation.

Enjoy!

9974014R00036

Printed in Great Britain
by Amazon.co.uk, Ltd.,
Marston Gate.